WHAT IS
ROSH HASHANAH?

WRITTEN BY
SHARI LAST

JEWISH NEW YEAR

What do you know about Rosh Hashanah?

Rosh Hashanah marks the beginning of the Jewish new year. Jewish people look to the year ahead and think about what's important to them. They pray for everything they want the next year to bring.

I'm sure many kids out there will have a whole LIST of things they want – a new bike, a cool holiday, the latest video game – but Rosh Hashanah is more about meaningful and spiritual things. Things like health, happiness, friendship, and success – which I'm sure you'll agree are all very important too!

There are no big parties, confetti, or fireworks on Rosh Hashanah, but there are plenty of traditions that make this holiday super fun!

LET'S FIND OUT MORE ABOUT ROSH HASHANAH!

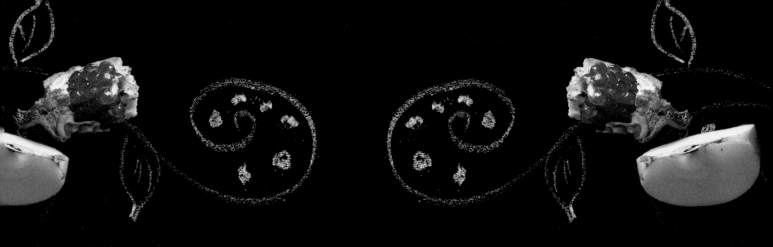

WHEN IS ROSH HASHANAH?

It's the new year, so Rosh Hashanah takes place on the first two days of the first month of the Hebrew calendar - the month of Tishri.

The Hebrew calendar is lunar, so it is different to the "regular" calendar. That's why Rosh Hashanah is not on the first of January – it's usually sometime in September.

Here is how Rosh Hashanah is written in Hebrew:

ראש השנה

HAPPY BIRTHDAY, WORLD!

Rosh Hashanah is a very special day - it is the anniversary of the creation of the world. According to Jewish history, the world was created less than 6,000 years ago.

WHAT'S IN A NAME?

In Hebrew, *Rosh Hashanah* means "head of the year", as in the new year. There are other names for this festival too: The Day of Judgement, the Day of Remembrance, and the Day of Blasting. (The blasting refers to the sound of the shofar, which we will learn about soon!)

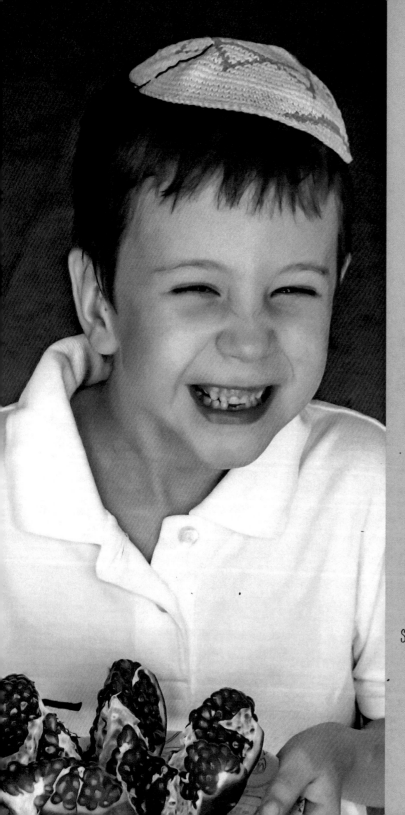

Joyful thoughts

A DAY OF CELEBRATION

Rosh Hashanah is a happy festival that celebrates the wonderful world we live in. Think about how incredible nature is! Marvel at the vastness of space! Celebrate your amazing human body! On Rosh Hashanah, Jewish people thank God for the world and praise Him for creating it in all its glory.

Family meals

Seeing friends *New clothes* *Sweet foods*

A DAY OF JUDGEMENT

It is also a serious day. We celebrate the world, but it's a meaningful celebration. We have a responsibility to inhabit this world kindly. As the new year begins, God looks at each person, one by one. He sees everything they've done and want to do. He knows everything they think and feel. He chooses what will happen to them over the coming year.

Reflection

Thinking about spiritual things

Prayer

Asking for a good year

THE HIGH HOLY DAYS

Rosh Hashanah marks the beginning of the High Holy Days, which end ten days later on Yom Kippur. Jewish people believe that during these ten days, God decides what will happen to each and every person in the coming year.

PREPARATION
The weeks before Rosh Hashanah are a time for reflection. Jewish people ask friends and family for forgiveness for anything they may have done wrong in the past year.

JUDGEMENT DAY

Rosh Hashanah is known as the Day of Judgement because God judges everyone's actions and behaviour from the past year. He uses this to decide how the coming year will go.

Shofar
Learn more about this instrument on the next page!

PRAYER

We pray a LOT on Rosh Hashanah – mostly that God should judge us kindly. Many of the prayers focus on how great, powerful, merciful, and kind God is.

GRATITUDE

Although Rosh Hashanah is about judgement, it is a joyous festival. We celebrate the world, God, and how lucky we are to have what we've got.

CELEBRATING ROSH HASHANAH

Rosh Hashanah is two days long. On these days, Jewish people are not supposed to do any work. This includes driving, cooking, writing, working, going to school, spending money, or using electronic devices. Instead, they spend time with family and friends and go to synagogue. They also . . .

DIP THE APPLE IN THE HONEY

One of the best-known things about Rosh Hashanah is dipping apples in honey. This can be done at any point during Rosh Hashanah, but many do it at the meal on the first night. A blessing is said and the apple and honey are eaten to symbolise our hopes for a sweet new year.

BLOW THE SHOFAR

The shofar is a sort of trumpet made from the horn of a kosher animal, usually a ram. It is blown 100 times on each day of Rosh Hashanah, during the prayer service. Every single person is supposed to hear all 100 blasts!

It's quite tricky to blow the shofar, but if you scrunch your mouth up just right, you might be able to!

EAT FESTIVE MEALS

Families sit down to big, festive meals over Rosh Hashanah. Each meal begins with a blessing over wine, then a blessing over challah. Lots of unusual foods are eaten at these Rosh Hashanah meals. Keep reading to find out more!

THE SHOFAR

In ancient times, the Jewish people would blow the shofar to mark important occasions. The noises it makes sound a bit like crying. It is supposed to remind us to think about the things we've done wrong and say sorry for them.

DID YOU KNOW?

Three notes are blown on the shofar: Tekiah, Shevarim, and Teruah.

Tekiah is one long blast.

Shevarim is three short blasts.

Teruah is at least nine very short blasts.

PRAYER

Rosh Hashanah is all about praying for a happy and sweet year ahead. Kids are encouraged to pray because our voices are important too. We read from a special prayer book called a *machzor*, and there are often fun children's services where we play games and eat snacks!

TEKIAH! SHEVARIM! TERUAH!

Luckily, kids don't have to blow the shofar 100 times on each day of Rosh Hashanah. There is someone who does it for the whole synagogue to hear. He is called the *baal tekiah*, and I'm sure he does lots of training beforehand!

TASHLICH

In the afternoon, there's a special prayer to "throw away" all our sins. To do this, we stand near a river, stream, or ocean and let our sins float away. Some people throw bread into the water to symbolise the sins.

THE SIMANIM

On the first night of Rosh Hashanah, it's traditional to start the festive meal with symbolic foods, known as *simanim*. Each of the *simanim* symbolises a specific blessing for the year ahead.

APPLE AND HONEY

For a sweet new year.

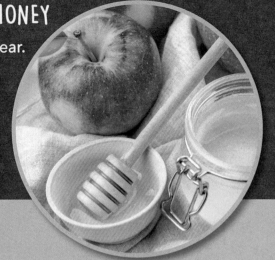

LEEKS

For enemies to be cut off.

The Hebrew word for "leek" is similar to the word for "cut."

DID YOU KNOW?

Some families go through all the *simanim* and say blessings, while others don't do any! Some stick to the most common ones: apples and honey, and pomegranate.

CARROTS

For blessings that grow as well as carrots do.

POMEGRANATES

For as many good deeds and rewards as the seeds of a pomegranate.

BEANS

For a fruitful year filled with goodness.

PUMPKINS

For bad decrees to be torn up, and good decrees to be announced.

FISH HEAD

We should be like the head of the fish . . . not the tail.

Some people eat from the fish head, while others just place it on the table!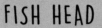

DATES

For enemies to be finished.

BEETROOT

For enemies to be removed.

NEW FRUIT

Another tradition is to eat new fruit. This is often done on the second night of Rosh Hashanah.

As we bring in the new year, we want to make a special blessing on something new, but we can only make it on something we haven't done or eaten in the past year. So we find a new fruit and make the blessing on it.

KIWI

YELLOW PITAYA

LYCHEE

Which ones have YOU tried?

DRAGON FRUIT

FEIJOA

Pomegranates used to be the new fruit everyone would eat. But now it is common to eat pomegranates throughout the year – so the hunt for more and more unusual fruits begins!

POMEGRANATE

BLOOD ORANGE

PASSION FRUIT

RAMBUTAN

COCONUT

FRUIT PARTY

My family tradition is to have a fruit party on the second night of Rosh Hashanah. We find as many unusual fruits as we can and taste them. Once, we had a fruit that tasted like custard, and another that made our mouths go dry!

TRADITIONAL FOODS
FOR A SWEET NEW YEAR

HONEY CAKE

A sweet, sticky honey cake is a traditional Rosh Hashanah food, and a delicious symbol of the sweet new year we are hoping for.

TZIMMES

Tzimmes is a traditional eastern-European dish of carrots (and sometimes prunes) stewed in honey.

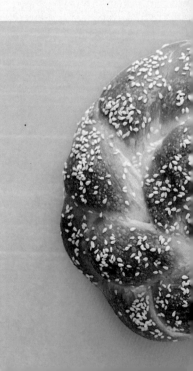

DRIED FRUIT

Platters of dried fruit are a popular Rosh Hashanah gift. This is because dried fruit is extra sweet!

ROUND CHALLAH

It's traditional to eat round challah on Rosh Hashanah because it symbolises the circle of life. Rosh Hashanah challahs are often sweet, either with raisins in the dough or a honey glaze. It is eaten dipped in honey.

HONEY

You might have noticed a theme: honey! Honey is used a LOT on Rosh Hashanah – because we are hoping for a sweet new year.

AROUND THE WORLD

There are a lot of unique Jewish communities around the world, and many of them have their own Rosh Hashanah traditions. Let's find out more!

DJERBA

Children on this Tunisian island gather fresh olives before Rosh Hashanah. They march through the streets on Rosh Hashanah morning, calling out the blessing that their good deeds should multiply like olive trees!

UKRAINE

A famous Hassidic rabbi is buried in a town called Uman in the Ukraine. Every year, thousands of Hassidic Jews travel there to spend Rosh Hashanah near him.

WESTERN EUROPE

It is traditional to settle all your debts and bills so you can start the new year with a clean slate.

TURKEY

Turkish Jews save some matzah from Passover and eat it on Rosh Hashanah. Just as the Jews were saved on Passover, so we should be saved from a bad decree on Rosh Hashanah.

ETHIOPIA

Some Ethiopian Jews dip their bodies in water before Rosh Hashanah and dress in white clothing to be as pure as can be when the new year begins.

ARGENTINA

A recent Rosh Hashanah tradition in Buenos Aires is the Urbano festival. It is open to the public and includes family activities, food, and speeches to celebrate Rosh Hashanah. Argentina has the largest Jewish population in South America, and Urbano can attract as many as 40,000 people!

IRAQ

Instead of a fish head, many Iraqi Jews place a ram's head on their Rosh Hashanah table. This symbolises the same thing as a fish head: the hope that we should be like the head and not the tail.

EASTERN EUROPE

Some Hassidic families buy new knives for every family member before Rosh Hashanah. This symbolises the wish for a plentiful year.

ROSH HASHANAH GREETINGS

If you have any Jewish friends and you want to wish them a happy Rosh Hashanah, here are a few ways to say it:

"HAPPY ROSH HASHANAH!"

"SHANAH TOVAH!"

Pronunciation: *Shuh-nuh Toh-vuh*
Hebrew meaning: "Have a good year!"

"SHANAH TOVAH UMETUKAH!"

Pronunciation: *Shuh-nuh Toh-vuh Oo-meh-took-uh*
Hebrew meaning: "Have a good and sweet year!"

"CHAG SAMEACH!"

Pronunciation: *Khuh-g Sum-ay-ukh*
Hebrew meaning: "Happy festival!"

"GMAR CHATIMAH TOVAH!"

Pronunciation: *Geh-marr Khut-im-uh Toh-vuh*
Hebrew meaning: "Good final sealing!"
It refers to having a good decree written and sealed for you.

NOTE
The "kh" sound in "Chag", "Sameach", and "Chatimah" is a guttural sound you make at the back of your throat. Or you can just use an "h" sound.

YOM KIPPUR

Yom Kippur is the final day of the High Holy Days. It is much more serious than Rosh Hashanah. Yom Kippur is when God finalises all the decisions made on Rosh Hashanah. It is a spiritual day, full of praying and thinking. We say sorry for our sins and beg God to forgive us.

It's traditional to wear white on Yom Kippur as a sign of purity.

Forgiveness

Before Rosh Hashanah, Jewish people ask each other for forgiveness. On Yom Kippur, they ask God for *His* forgiveness.

A fast day

On Yom Kippur, adults (and boys aged 13+ and girls aged 12+) fast for 25 hours from sundown until nightfall the next day. This is so we don't focus on physical things like food – but on more spiritual matters.

A long day

Most Jewish festivals include big family meals – but not Yom Kippur. As it's an important fast day, people spend most of it in synagogue. Kids sometimes go home for a break in the middle.

Plenty of praying

On a regular weekday, there are three Jewish prayer services. On Shabbat and festivals, there are four. On Yom Kippur ... there are FIVE!

Kids in synagogue

Although we spend most of Yom Kippur in synagogue where adults pray a LOT, there are usually fun prayer services for younger kids, and sometimes a lunch for children who are too young to fast.

Mercy please

Many of the prayers of Yom Kippur refer to stories from the Torah where God showed mercy to people who did something wrong.

LET'S MAKE HONEY CAKE!

This recipe requires an electric mixer or whisk and a bit of patience, but it makes the most delicious, sticky but light, honey cake! These ingredients will make two long loaves.

Ingredients

- 2 eggs
- 1 cup sugar
- 1/2 cup oil
- 1/2 jar honey (225g jar)
- 1 cup self-raising flour
- 1 cup plain flour
- 1/2 tsp baking soda
- 1 tsp cinnamon
- 1/2 tbsp cocoa
- 1/2 tsp coffee powder
- 1 cup boiling water

Method

1. Turn on the oven to 175°C (350°F).
2. Beat eggs and sugar very gradually until creamy.
3. Keep the mixer on and slowly add oil, then honey, also slowly.
4. In a separate bowl, mix flour, baking soda, cinnamon, cocoa, and coffee.
5. In batches, add the dry mix to the wet mixture. Make sure each batch is mixed in before adding the next.
6. Slowly add the boiling water while mixing continuously.
7. Pour into two long loaf tins and bake for around 40 minutes, or until a toothpick comes out of the cake clean.

Cut into slices, honey cake is perfect for a breakfast treat!

Some people like to top their cake with nuts. Try pistachios, cashews, or almonds.

What about some frosting? A simple mixture of boiling water and icing sugar will do.

Candied fruit is another topping idea - if you want to add some zing to the flavour!

ROSH HASHANAH CRAFT IDEAS

POMEGRANATE STAMPS

Create some decorative artwork using one of Rosh Hashanah's symbolic foods. Ask an adult to help you cut a pomegranate in half – careful, it might splash!. Dip it in paint and stamp away!

Use other fruit or colours to make different patterns. What will you choose?

FESTIVE TABLE SETTINGS

Make your Rosh Hashanah table special. Think of what you could add to each table setting. Individual honey dishes? Small cups for the blessing over wine? (Don't worry, kids can drink grape juice!) Maybe you can use apples as placecards – or even as the centrepiece!

PERFECT PROPS

There are lots of symbolic foods and special items that are used on Rosh Hashanah. From the shofar and fish to apples, pomegranates, and new fruits. Draw or paint some Rosh Hashanah objects, cut them out, and attach them to sticks. You can hand these out at the festive meals.

HAPPY BEES

Rosh Hashanah is all about honey, right? It's the ultimate symbol for a sweet new year. Let's build some bees from card and coloured paper. Used them to decorate your home or give out as Rosh Hashanah greetings to your friends.

What will you use to craft the wings, eyes, and antennae?

First published in Great Britain in 2024
by **TELL ME MORE** Books

Text copyright ©2024 Shari Last
Design copyright ©2024 Shari Last

ISBN: 978-1-917200-03-5

Picture credits: Thanks to Adobe Stock;
Ale Vega, Annie Spratt, Lavi Perchik, Tim Marshall,
Wout Vanacker, and Yulia Khlebnikova at Unsplash;
and Chameleons Eye, Inna Reznick, John Theodor, Lisa-skvo,
Paulaphoto, Pixel-Shot, Roman Yanushevsky, Tomertu,
and Valerii Sokolovskyi at Shutterstock.com.

WWW.TELLMEMOREBOOKS.COM

Made in United States
North Haven, CT
16 August 2024